Words to Live By

Kate and Emily Marshall

BROADWAY BOOKS · NEW YORK

Words to Live By

A Journal of Wisdom
for Someone You Love

Broadway Books titles may be purchased for business or promotional use or for special sales. For information, please write to: Special Markets Department, Random House, Inc., 1745 Broadway, New York, NY 10019.

PRINTED IN THE UNITED STATES OF AMERICA

BROADWAY BOOKS and its logo, a letter B bisected on the diagonal, are trademarks of Random House, Inc.

Visit our Web site at www.broadwaybooks.com

First edition published 2005

Book design by Caroline Cunningham

ISBN 0-7679-1909-2

1 3 5 7 9 10 8 6 4 2

A collection of thoughts for

Marty Cowan

Presented on

Your 35th Birthday
with love,
Laurie

We have no greater gift to offer than what we ourselves

have learned through trial and error, luck, hard work, false starts,

dream-chasing, and living life. This is a collection of the lessons we've

learned, and of our ideas and thoughts on leading a full and happy life.

We don't claim to have all the answers,

but we have discovered a few things along the way

that we want to share with you.

... for you to pass along to your handsome sons when the time is right.

Contributors to this journal

or

Opening remarks

Contents

～

Words to
Live By

Introduction

The first time my daughter, Emily, drove off in the family car by herself, the ink on her driver's license not yet dry, I took a deep breath and prayed that the driving school and I had taught her well. A year later, when it finally sank in that in order to go to college she'd have to leave home, I reminded myself that my job as a parent has been to give her the tools to succeed and then let her go. Even so, I admit that I worried: Did I forget to teach her something important? Was I done?

For years I've been thinking about when Emily and her younger brother, Ben, leave home for good. Will they be happy? Will they love their jobs? Will they be money-wise? Will they find love? Will they eat their vegetables? I hope that when they head off into the world, they will be ready. It's not that I have all the answers or that they couldn't find their own ways, far from it. But when Emily and Ben leave the nest, I want them to go with the counsel of loved ones.

Emily and Ben know that their family elders have learned a few things about life. The diversity of our styles, interests, and appetites makes for a wonderfully rich blend of insights and talents. For instance, their seventy-seven-year-old grandmother keeps herself mentally and physically fit by traveling the country competing in herding trials with her eager border collies. One of their uncles, president of Ben & Jerry's for many years, works to make "business ethics" real. One generous grandfather has tirelessly volunteered in his community all his life. Other relatives have been strong and wise enough to find happiness in some unusual ways. They all have something to teach, be it about love, money, good health, or even how to make people laugh.

Bits of this advice come out when we assemble as a family on holidays or at reunions, but to be honest, much of it doesn't. Life lessons don't necessarily come up naturally. No one ever asks, "Would you like some pie . . . and the secret to a happy marriage?"

After deciding on a college, Emily began feeling the excitement and nervousness that come with leaving home and the idea of being on her own. I started thinking about how to mark the occasion of her high-school-to-college transition in a personal way. I wanted her to know that her family will always be here for her, ready to share what we know about life, when she wants to hear it.

While brainstorming ways to tap some of her family's insights about issues she may not be sure how to bring up or may not have specific questions about yet, we came up with the idea of an advice journal to collect the varied and valuable wisdom of the people important to her. Emily and I cowrote the journal with questions that satisfied both her wish for adult-to-adult dialogue and my parental instincts.

Other family members were pleased to be given a way to help celebrate her life transition and to show their ongoing support. Some wrote in the journal while visiting us. Others e-mailed us bits to paste in. We snail-mailed it to a few long-distance relatives for some wonderful handwritten entries. I kept notes on what I wanted to say and wrote them in at the end. Soon the journal was full of life lessons and advice. We presented it to Emily as a high school graduation gift.

We all feel good about Emily taking the wisdom of several generations with her to a new life in college and beyond. She is glad to have the journal's familiar voices with her while far from home. We also see the book as an invitation for Emily to talk with us more in depth about life issues as she experiences them in the future. Who knows, maybe she'll pass the journal along to her own daughter someday to show what her great-relatives had on their minds. We do know that we have started a new family tradition.

We offer you this fill-in version of *Words to Live By* for you to use as you wish. We encourage you to take this opportunity to share your wisdom with someone you love. Whether one person fills it out or many, we know it will be treasured.

How to Use This Journal

WHEN TO USE THIS JOURNAL

There are as many right times to use this journal as there are people who have lessons to teach and people who want to learn them. *Words to Live By* can be a heartfelt gift for any big moment in life, from heading off to college, boarding school, or military service to graduating from a school or program to having a milestone birthday (turning thirteen, sixteen, eighteen, twenty-one . . .) to a celebration of young adulthood (bar mitzvah, quinceañero, etc.) to a wedding, first job, first child, or other new beginning.

But you don't need to be celebrating a milestone to share wisdom. Writing down some hard-won life lessons is a great way to leave a footprint in the sand. You may want to use this journal on a visit with an aging relative to help you understand their values and record them for posterity, or as a tool to ask questions of someone whose life you admire and to honor that person's viewpoints. You may want to use it to chronicle your own views for clarity and insight into your own approach to life.

There is no one right way or one special occasion for using this journal. Trust yourself to know when to record your or someone else's views on living fully and beautifully. It could be at a big juncture in life or at a quiet, reflective time.

PLANNING THIS JOURNAL

Once you've decided to give this unique book to a loved one, you'll need to decide how you'd like to use it. Before you begin, determine how many contributors you want. Having lots of contributors can make for a rich variety of styles and viewpoints and can give a more complete picture of "the village" that raised the person getting the journal. On the other hand, a journal written just by parents or a favorite grandparent can allow these writers more space to express themselves in an intimate and personal way. Whichever you choose, make sure you allow plenty of time for contributors (yourself or a group) to fill in the advice. If you're giving this as a gift for a particular occasion, start well ahead of time, or give the gift with a promise to have it filled out within a certain time.

When thinking about whom to ask to contribute, think about whom the person ultimately receiving the journal would want to hear from most. You could ask them whom they would like to have contribute or you could surprise them. Besides key family members, are there others who have been important? Is there a neighbor who has been just like family? A teacher who made an impression? A scout leader or coach who really understood the person? Think about who is likely to have some interesting, funny, poignant, or opinionated entries and plan accordingly.

When asking for contributions, consider directing particular people to specific topics. If your brother has no money sense but has a loving thirty-year marriage, flag the section on relationships or e-mail the questions from that section to him. Likewise, steer your fitness-guru sister to the physical health section. But keep an open mind; inviting people to write in any section that inspires them will produce a colorful, interesting mix of advice.

Decide how much time you want to invest and how much control you need over this project to make it happen. Look at your list of desired contributors. How available are they? How close? Do they like to communicate in person or by phone, e-mail, or regular mail? Is there a procrastinator in the bunch or someone likely to forget this journal on a park bench? Fit your plan to your contributors.

Assure contributors that they don't need to be experts or have it all figured out in order to make a meaningful contribution. Some people may also be concerned about their handwriting. Either let them know that sloppy is fine (it adds character), or offer to paste in their typed entries. And if people have a lot to say, consider starting a second volume rather than limiting their space.

The number, distance, and preferences of your contributors will guide the approach you take to completing this journal. We suggest any of the following approaches.

Quick and Easy

Of course, if only one or two people from the same household are writing, it's simple. You can fill it out when you please. If the additional people you are asking to contribute are local, have them write in it the next time they stop by or loan them the journal for a weekend. Are any big family gatherings being planned, or could you initiate one? Pass the journal around at the next family event to complete it in one fell swoop. Let people know in advance if you want well-thought-out entries, or surprise them to get more spontaneous responses.

When Contributors Are Distant or Busy

In these cases, use e-mail to request responses. E-mail usually gets quick responses and works well with long-distance or busy contributors. Send some suggested topics, then paste or hand-copy their responses into the journal. If you have people who prefer talking to writing, interview them in person or by phone and record their responses.

If You Have Time

A terrific way to personalize the journal is to send the journal on a house-to-house adventure. Send it to the first person along with a list of other participants and instructions on where to send it next. Consider including stamped and addressed mailing envelopes to keep it moving. This way takes a little more time and follow-up, but you end up with a tapestry of well-thought-out entries in each contributor's own handwriting.

Any of these approaches work. Whether you have ten people giving advice over Thanksgiving dinner or two parents lovingly filling out entries at bedtime, the result will certainly be a caring and heartfelt gift.

TIPS FOR WRITING IN THIS JOURNAL

You have found a wonderful way to support someone embarking on a new life. This journal will be a very personal and appreciated gift. *Words to Live By* is designed to help you share your advice, thoughts, favorite sayings, or quotes on a variety of life themes with someone special to you. The complete journal will be enjoyed as a collection of lessons learned from cherished friends and family.

Take Your Time. Don't try to rush through this. It is a one-of-a-kind gift and will require some thought. It may help to keep notes throughout the day as ideas of what you want to say start percolating. When you're ready to start writing, sit down with a cup of tea, away from the phone and other distractions, and begin. If you find yourself tiring, set it aside and continue later. If there are other contributors, write your name and the date after each entry.

Say only as much as you have to say. You don't have to write on every topic or fill every page. Your advice will be most authentic and helpful when it's something you feel strongly about, so feel free to skip categories that don't inspire you. Write as much or as little as you feel is necessary. We may have provided a full page for a topic, but if you feel that a one-sentence response does the job, that's fine. If you need more room or have something to say outside of the categories or top-ics we have offered, use the "Other" pages at the end of each section or at the end of the journal.

Speak from the heart. Don't censor yourself or write just what you think people will expect to see or deem the "right" advice. There are hundreds of expert advice books out there. This jour-nal is different; it is created especially for your loved one by the people who know and love the recipient best. Some of the best tips for living come from hard-earned wisdom that may be star-tling or go against the grain. Work-in-progress wisdom works, too. If you're still fine-tuning your approach to, for example, balancing work and family, just tell it as you see it now. Be true and be yourself.

Embrace your mistakes. A lot of life lessons are won the hard way. Some of the most memorable stories are the ones in which someone messes up but learns and ends up the better for it. When someone we know and respect tells such a tale about him-self, the moral is all the more personal and powerful. Honor the times you stumbled and learned from it by sharing the story. Many people appreciate this humble approach to teaching instead of a lecture.

Draw from any source you choose. If you are inspired to pen an original masterpiece, go for it. But also feel free to quote favorite leaders or comedians, or to borrow lines from songs, scripture, movies, or even television shows. Use any voice that expresses your point of view and that you think is good advice.

Say it your way. If you have something profound to say, say it, but simple truths can pack a punch, too. If humor is your style, say it that way. You can be philosophical (e.g., "True success is only achieved honestly") or be downright practical (e.g., "Balance your checkbook every month"). If you believe it is important to good living, it belongs. There is no wrong style and there are no wrong answers.

Sit down, relax, and be generous with your thoughts and wisdom. As with most gifts, the giver is made richer for the giving. As you reflect and write on various life topics, you might find yourself rededicating yourself to following your own good advice. And you will surely feel good about passing on a few words to live by.

Mind

~

An Active, Happy Mind

$\mathcal{I}$'d describe a healthy mind as one that:

Keep your mind fit and active all your life by:

You might find these classes or activities interesting at some time in your life:

_____

_____

_____

_____

_____

_____

_____

Some reading I've gotten a lot out of that you might too is:

_____

_____

_____

_____

_____

_____

_____

_____

_____

You'll laugh a lot in life if you:

$\mathcal{I}$ think people with good judgment, intelligence, or "people smarts" got that way by:

_____

_____

_____

_____

_____

_____

_____

$\mathcal{A}$ good "support system" for your well-being includes:

_____

_____

_____

_____

_____

_____

_____

_____

Here is how I've learned the way people keep a positive attitude, and how it helps them:

$\mathcal{T}$his person has been one of my role models because:

*P*eople who deal well with conflict, anger, fear, or other strong emotions seem to do it by:

$\mathcal{T}$his can be a great way to let off stress:

When you're lonely, down, or have lost something important to you, try this:

Specific things that I usually find comforting (particular foods, activities, or other) are:

_____

_____

_____

_____

_____

_____

_____

_____

_____

_____

_____

_____

_____

_____

_____

_____

_____

_____

_____

_____

_____

*O*verall, I'd say people are happy when they:

*O*ther thoughts on an active, happy mind:

Body

An Apple a Day . . .

Healthy eating means:

Here are a few tried-and-true tips for cooking wholesome foods or making healthy choices when eating out:

One of the best-tasting nutritious meals I know (and the recipe) is:

The best way to stay fit is to:

*T*hese exercise "dos and don'ts" make good sense:

$\mathcal{I}$ like these skin care, makeup, and/or hair care tips for beauty or health:

These home remedies, herbs, or alternative medicines often work for:

_____

_____

_____

_____

_____

_____

_____

_____

Watch for these family medical issues (that can be inherited):

_____

_____

_____

_____

_____

_____

_____

_____

My view on drug, tobacco, and alcohol use is:

These are my thoughts on health insurance and getting the most from your health care providers:

The key to feeling more rested and energetic is to:

The secret to aging well is:

Overall, the key to good health is:

$\mathcal{O}$ther thoughts on a healthy body:

Spirit

Your Spiritual Life

Being spiritual means:

$\mathcal{S}$piritual faith is found and nurtured by:

Prayer, worship, and meditation can play this role in your life:

_____

_____

_____

_____

_____

_____

_____

A good place or person to go to for spiritual guidance is:

_____

_____

_____

_____

_____

_____

_____

_____

_____

When your faith is shaken, try this:

When you choose a place of worship, consider:

These books, poems, movies, or songs may give you insights about spirituality:

_____

_____

_____

_____

_____

_____

_____

_____

One of my favorite sayings, scripture passages, or prayers (and when I use it) is:

_____

_____

_____

_____

_____

_____

_____

_____

_____

These traditions and rituals have been meaningful or comforting to me:

A moral or virtuous person is someone who:

$\mathcal{S}$ome less obvious ways or places to care for your spirit are:

_____

_____

_____

_____

_____

_____

_____

_____

$\mathcal{W}$hen you relate to people of other faiths, remember that:

_____

_____

_____

_____

_____

_____

_____

_____

_____

*O*ther thoughts on your spiritual life:

Recreation

The Lighter Side of Life

$\mathcal{I}$ recommend this satisfying hobby:

_____
_____
_____
_____
_____
_____
_____
_____

$\mathcal{A}$ good sport to do or cheer for is:

_____
_____
_____
_____
_____
_____
_____
_____
_____
_____

*T*hese are some inexpensive ways to have fun:

My idea of a great day or evening is:

_____

_____

_____

_____

_____

_____

_____

_____

My favorite way to relax is to:

_____

_____

_____

_____

_____

_____

_____

_____

$\mathcal{A}$n enjoyable way to bring out your creative side is to:

_____

_____

_____

_____

_____

_____

_____

_____

$\mathcal{I}$ highly recommend these movies or shows and these books or authors:

_____

_____

_____

_____

_____

_____

_____

_____

_____

*T*hese are outstanding musicians or songs you may enjoy sometime:

_____

_____

_____

_____

_____

_____

_____

A wonderful vacation is:

_____

_____

_____

_____

_____

_____

_____

_____

_____

Here are some of my "bests" (best city to visit, beach, shopping, museum, camping site, restaurant, golf course, resort, singles' hot spot, place for family fun, or other):

The key to being a good traveler or trip planner is:

I like this funny little joke or story:

$\mathcal{O}$ther thoughts on the lighter side of life:

Friendship

The Art of Making and Keeping Friends

These are the qualities I look for in a friend:

You can be a good friend to someone else by:

$\mathcal{S}$ome ideas for making or deepening friendships are:

$\mathcal{I}$n my experience, lasting friendships come from:

This is something that often strains friendships, and my
view on how to resolve it:

$\mathcal{I}$f a friend is not treating you right, I suggest:

$\mathcal{I}$f being truthful would hurt a friend's feelings, I think it's best to:

_____

_____

_____

_____

_____

_____

_____

$\mathcal{P}$olitics, religion, and other controversial subjects among friends are:

_____

_____

_____

_____

_____

_____

_____

_____

*P*ets as friends are:

_____

_____

_____

_____

_____

_____

_____

I consider this person my good friend because:

_____

_____

_____

_____

_____

_____

_____

_____

_____

$\mathcal{O}$ther thoughts on the art of making and keeping friends:

Love

~~

Finding and Sharing Love

The difference between men and women is:

$\mathcal{S}$ingle life can be satisfying if you:

My thoughts on dating and looking for the right guy or girl (meeting and attracting someone, first dates, blind dates, playing the field, etc.) are:

_____

_____

_____

_____

_____

_____

_____

_____

_____

_____

_____

_____

_____

_____

_____

_____

_____

_____

_____

_____

*O*nce you've found someone special, keep him or her by:

When you need to end a relationship or when your own heart is broken, I suggest:

You know you are in love when:

*B*efore committing to or marrying someone, think about these things:

These are the characteristics of a good relationship or marriage:

_____

_____

_____

_____

_____

_____

_____

I think these people make a great couple because:

_____

_____

_____

_____

_____

_____

_____

_____

_____

I think loving relationships last when:

Here are some tips on handling specific challenges (money, chores, jealousy, or others):

$\mathcal{I}$n my experience, couples who handle disagreements well
do it by:

$\mathcal{I}$f times get really tough between you and your mate,
I suggest:

$\mathcal{A}$s you age, love becomes:

*O*ther thoughts on finding and sharing love:

Parenting

~

Nurturing Children

This is a great way to support or nurture children (even if you aren't a parent yourself):

*O*verall, being a father or mother is:

When thinking about if or when to have your own children, consider:

The basic task of parenting is to:

*C*ommunicating with children and teens seems to work best
when:

Kids feel secure and loved when you:

If you teach just one value, insight, or skill to children, it should be:

_____

_____

_____

_____

_____

_____

_____

_____

Some of the best children's books, toys, games, or activities are:

_____

_____

_____

_____

_____

_____

_____

Help a child discover and develop special talents by:

This is a common parenting problem, and my suggestions for how to handle it:

When feeling stressed or overwhelmed by parenting, it helps to:

$\mathcal{O}$ther thoughts on nurturing children:

Money

~

Developing Money Smarts

$\mathcal{I}$n my experience, money plays this role in people's overall well-being:

_____

_____

_____

_____

_____

_____

_____

_____

_____

_____

_____

_____

_____

_____

_____

_____

_____

_____

$\mathcal{H}$ere is how to avoid money conflicts with family or friends:

These are some common money mistakes:

The key to spending less than you earn is to:

Smart shoppers use these techniques:

_____

_____

_____

_____

_____

_____

_____

The trick to using credit cards, ATMs, or other ready-money
wisely is:

_____

_____

_____

_____

_____

_____

_____

_____

Some rules of thumb about car, home, or other insurance
are:

My advice on taxes (saving on, paying for, or filing them) is:

When you're young, keep these kinds of financial accounts
and manage them by:

$\mathcal{S}$ome general principles of smart investing are:

Some tips for buying a car or a house are:

My thoughts on what you need to save for, how much you need, and how to do it are:

My thoughts on giving to charity are:

_____

_____

_____

_____

_____

_____

_____

Some good places for information and advice about money
matters are:

_____

_____

_____

_____

_____

_____

_____

_____

$\mathcal{O}$ther thoughts on developing money smarts:

Work

~

A Satisfying Work Life

$\mathcal{W}$hen deciding what kind of work to do, consider:

You will enjoy your work and accomplish much if you:

$\mathcal{I}$n my opinion, jobs or careers to pursue (or not) are:

_____

_____

_____

_____

_____

_____

_____

_____

$\mathcal{T}$hese skills are useful for practically any job:

_____

_____

_____

_____

_____

_____

_____

_____

_____

Here are some job-hunting tips:

If you are starting out with little or no experience, it helps to:

$\mathcal{S}$ome tips on teamwork, time management, leadership, or other important skills are:

This is my idea of a great boss, coworker, or employee:

My advice for working with difficult bosses, coworkers, or employees is:

If you are unhappy in your job or career, think about:

My ideas on balancing work, recreation, and family are:

Other thoughts on a satisfying work life:

Citizenship

~

Making a Difference

$\mathcal{O}$ur responsibility as citizens (local, national, or world) is to:

$\mathcal{I}$ respect this person or group for making an important contribution to society:

Rights and principles to cherish and causes worth standing up for are:

These are outstanding activities or groups to donate your time or money to:

Stay informed about important issues by:

When deciding which political or other type of leader to
support, consider:

If you think something in your community or beyond needs changing or improving, I suggest:

_____

_____

_____

_____

_____

_____

_____

_____

_____

_____

_____

_____

_____

_____

_____

_____

_____

_____

The best way to take a stand on an issue and to bring about the change you want is to:

*O*ur world could be better if:

Other thoughts on making a difference:

Success

A Life Well Lived

$\mathcal{I}$ would define success as:

T he way I look at failure is:

$\mathcal{I}$f there is a formula for becoming successful, it is:

$\mathcal{S}$uccessful people tend to have these personal qualities:

If you could choose just one area of your life to succeed in, choose:

_____

_____

_____

_____

_____

_____

_____

This person is a hero or mentor of mine because:

_____

_____

_____

_____

_____

_____

_____

_____

_____

This is one of my favorite success stories:

$\mathcal{A}$ life is well lived if:

*O*ther thoughts on a life well lived:

Other

A Few More Things . . .

Here are a few more things I'd like to say to you that didn't seem to belong in any other section, or that I ran out of room for elsewhere:

Invitation

Are you particularly proud of an entry in this journal? Is there an entry you would like to share with the world? If so, we invite you to mail it to us for possible inclusion in a later volume of homespun wisdom.

Send us:
- your written entry (original works only!)
- your name, address, and e-mail address (important so we can contact you before reprinting your entry)
- another tidbit about yourself: your age? profession? number of grandchildren? relationship to the person you wrote it for?

Mail to:

Kate & Emily Marshall
Words to Live By
P.O. Box 6846
Moraga, CA 94570-6846